What I Know

I KNOW THINGS THAT GO

By Trisha James

Gareth Stevens PUBLISHING

first concepts

I know things that go.
This is a bicycle.

This is a scooter.

This is a car.

This is a truck.

This is a tractor.

This is a motorcycle.

POLICE
111
POLICE

This is a bus.

SCHOOL BUS
STOP

This is a boat.

This is an airplane.

This is a train.

800
800
B&O

Which way to go
do you like best?

SCHOOL BUS

800

Please visit our website, www.garethstevens.com. For a free color catalog of all our high-quality books, call toll free 1-800-542-2595 or fax 1-877-542-2596.

Cataloging-in-Publication Data

Names: James, Trisha.
Title: I know things that go / Trisha James.
Description: New York : Gareth Stevens Publishing, 2018. | Series: What I know
Identifiers: ISBN 9781482463095 (pbk.) | ISBN 9781482463118 (library bound) | ISBN 9781482463101 (6 pack)
Subjects: LCSH: Transportation–Juvenile literature. | Vehicles–Juvenile literature.
Classification: LCC TL147.J36 2017 | DDC 629.04–dc23

First Edition

Published in 2018 by
Gareth Stevens Publishing
111 East 14th Street, Suite 349
New York, NY 10003

Designer: Sarah Liddell
Editor: Therese Shea

Photo credits: Cover, p. 1 (stripes) Eky Studio/Shutterstock.com; cover, p. 1 (main) S_E/Shutterstock.com; pp. 3, 23 (bike) VisanuPhotoshop/Shutterstock.com; p. 5 Romrodphoto/Shutterstock.com; p. 7 Peter38/Shutterstock.com; p. 9 Mike Flippo/Shutterstock.com; p. 11 Fotokostic/Shutterstock.com; p. 13 Philip Lange/Shutterstock.com; pp. 15, 23 (bus) Stuart Monk/Shutterstock.com; p. 17 Italianvideoagency/Shutterstock.com; pp. 19, 23 (airplane) IM_photo/Shutterstock.com; pp. 21, 23 (train) Kenneth Sponsler/Shutterstock.com.

Printed in the United States of America

CPSIA compliance information: Batch #CS17GS: For further information contact Gareth Stevens, New York, New York at 1-800-542-2595.

What I Know

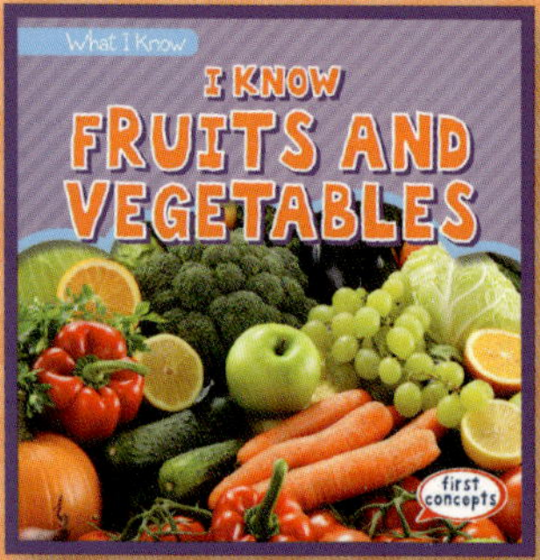

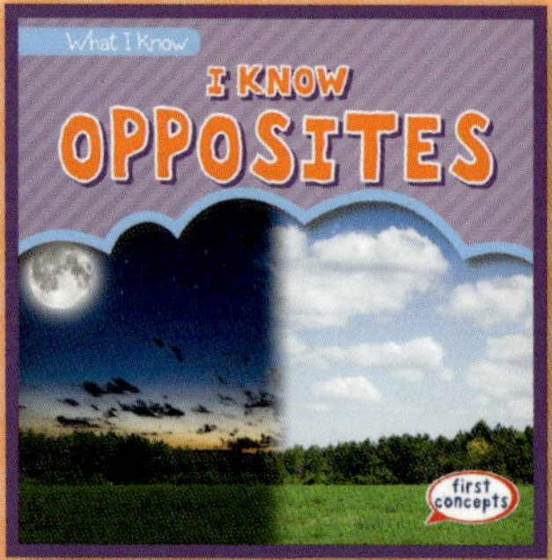

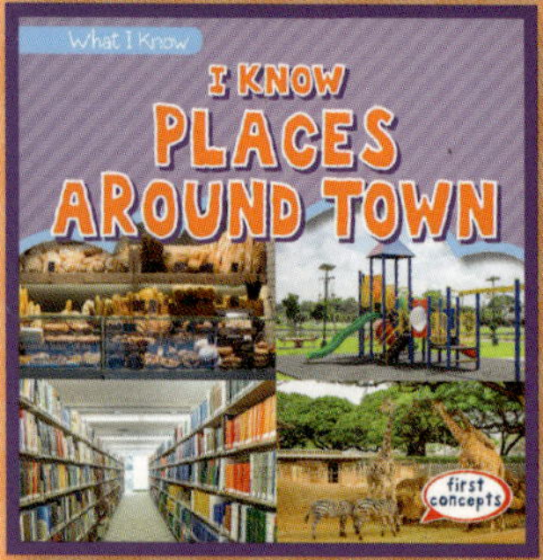

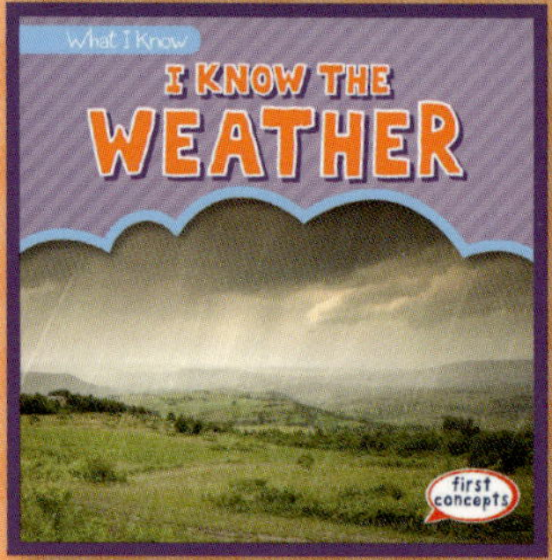

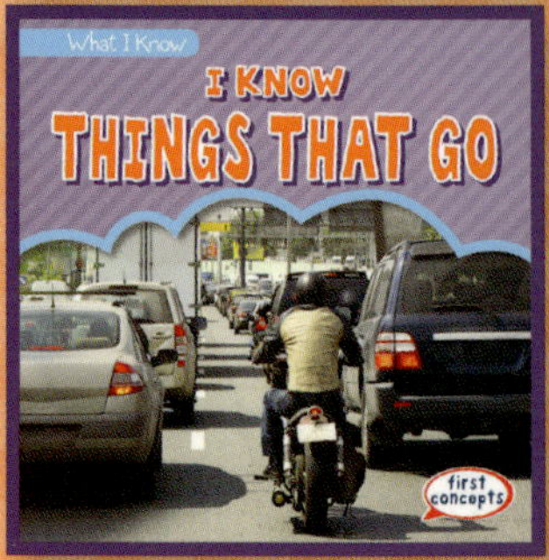

Levels: GR: B; DRA: 2

ISBN: 9781482463095
6-pack ISBN: 9781482463101
9 781482 463095

Gareth Stevens
PUBLISHING